Journey to Your Center Oracle

Jackie Smith-Jefferson

BALBOA.PRESS
A DIVISION OF HAY HOUSE

Balboa Press books may be ordered through booksellers or by contacting:

Balboa Press
A Division of Hay House
1663 Liberty Drive
Bloomington, IN 47403
www.balboapress.com
844-682-1282

ISBN: 978-1-9822-5860-3 (sc)
ISBN: 978-1-9822-5861-0 (e)

Print information available on the last page.

Balboa Press rev. date: 01/08/2021

Preface

"IN EACH EXPERIENCE OF MY life, I have had to step out of one little space of the known light, into a large area of darkness. I had to stand awhile in the darkness, and then gradually God has given me light. But not to linger in. For as soon as that light has felt familiar, then the call has always come to step out ahead again into new darkness." _____ Mary McLeod Bethune

From the moment I read Dr Bethune's biography, I felt her call to go beyond my own perceived limitations. I could almost hear her say these words along my journey. Whenever she saw a need, she always found a way to meet that need and move closer to her vision. Throughout my life, I too saw darkness. But with darkness, when you become still and remember what you do know, your eyes adjust to see your way into the next room. She once said, without faith, nothing is possible. With it, nothing is impossible. Thank you, Dr. Bethune

Dedication

Dear Fellow Traveler,

I am so grateful you chose to consider this little book to accompany you on your journey. I hope you know how precious you are and how worthy you are of doing the work it takes to realize and to maintain your awareness of your true value.

My travels included being a mother to a beautiful. benevolent and innovative daughter, Audrey and a nana to her daughter, Grace, who is fearless and lives out the meaning of her name. They are my why.

This book and all my work are dedicated to lighting the way to a truer self, yours and mine. It is said that if you do not do your own emotional work, it will be left for your children and your children's children to finish it. That is a most distressing thought for me. I assume it affects you similarly.

While I'm at it, big love and a humble thanks to those who modeled how to live from gracious and hearty spirits; My funny, brilliant parents, Kitty and Smitty, who greeted and treated every life they encountered as if they mattered; My brothers and besties, Jay and J.C., whom I am proud to know, (even if they weren't kinfolk), practice husbands, my lover, (who helps me keep my heart open), beautiful bountiful Amazonian sisters who have all showed me the way to love, My teachers and mentors, while too many to count, I've got to give a special mention to Jackie Long, John Hatcher, Rudy S., Camille H., Diane K. S., Jan and Barry S., Umari Jutte, Mary Faulkner, Rev. Mitch Johnson, and other countless Angels, sisters and brothers along the way who continue to pour into me, have my back, be a witness, hold my hand, call my B.S., and be a cheerleader along the road less traveled! Through the consistent emotional challenges and growth, you are all my how. Thank you!

Introduction

DURING MY PERSONAL JOURNEY, I have felt at times alternately as if I were on an obstacle course, a target at the shooting range or stranded in the middle of a desert. My need in those moments were not to commiserate and tear at my breast singing in my Billie Holiday voice, "Sometimes, I feel like a motherless child"! But instead to be still and ground myself in truth and self-compassion. It is ideal for you and I, in all cases, to remember who we are at our core, a spiritual being. It is most effective to keep simple tools at our ready. As my mother would sometimes say, "When you got crocodiles (life) nipping at your ankles…" your prayer may end up being a one-word exclamation, i.e., HELP, versus a poetic verse from the book of Psalms! Hence, I will keep all things simple. It is also imperative that we keep touchstones, tokens and road markers close by to bring us back to a sense of safety, that which we believe to be true and values we hold as important. Also, in my journey, I have found that a good question, asked by a fellow traveler, to be most useful. It is my hope that this workbook may be a touchstone for you in your journey.

You may wonder why I use the term "Oracle". In classic antiquity it described a Priest or Priestess considered to have special powers of prophecy. It might also identify a place, or a shrine regarded as an authority or guide for someone seeking advice usually of a spiritual or serious life matter.

Early in my healing process, I sought for myself everywhere. Well, I knew I was searching for something. I did not know at the time what I searched for: Perhaps a feeling, a breakthrough, a revelation, the right church, a choir, a band, a drug, food, prophets, a different city, a relationship, a new profession. I was always seeking outside of myself. The answer all the while was within. The truth of my being is in my core. I am my oracle! You, Dear Heart, are your own Oracle!

The Journey to Your Center Oracle is a soul journey connecting you to your core where your truth resides, your Oracle. The journey offers tools to help you build the inner strength that living your truth requires. Your soul is directly connected to the Soul of the Universe. Take your time. Yes, study is useful! But more importantly, be present to the miracle that is your soul. It is imperative to develop this relationship. It is my hope that folks on all spiritual paths can use my little book as a tool in this endeavor of becoming our own Oracle!

Preparation

THE JOURNEY TO (AND FROM time to time, back to...) our center is a warrior's journey. Fraught with disappointments, wrong turns, attacks from within, and distractions from outside sources, that often turn out to be Godsequences. With Spirit to guide us, a mustard seed of faith, hope, and enough willingness to make one more step forward, we will see with our own eyes that we not only will survive but we will THRIVE!

The basis for the content of "The Journey to Your Center Oracle" workbook is centered around principles and tools accumulated over a seven-decade journey, including starts and stops, and a final jarring fall from grace. In a Godsequence way, it was the fall that led to a new consciousness, engaged in three decades of teaching. I had lost my way countless times on new issues and old issues on new levels. I realized I could no longer recite old scripts, stand on old beliefs, re-enact old and outdated patterns. I needed gas, not steam.

I have realized once you are awake, you can get stuck and waylaid, but you cannot turn back. The New Thought community, Unity Church principles, Twelve Step programs, and a multitude of supplemental sources of truth have blessed and prospered me with a richness of spirit I did not even imagine were attainable. I believe there are others like me that never give up. We are always ready to learn and grow. We may from time to time take "three steps forward and two steps back", but we "keep coming back" to our center. These tools are for us all, from all walks of life, all cultures, all spiritual and religious practices. As I was introduced to a new way of responding to life, I realized hope is not an emotion. It is a discipline. I am impelled to share the hope that showed the way for me.

What Lies Ahead

THERE ARE MANY WAYS TO use this workbook: It can be a compliment to your morning meditation, a journal exercise, a part of a 40-day centering challenge, a therapeutic group ritual with trusted friends, or warm-up toward deeper fellowship. Practice the use of your instincts to glean the message that spirit would have you focus on this leg of your journey.

The Journey to Your center involves thirty-six principles that create a process of self-examination, asking in depth questions to challenge your present mindset. There are no right or wrong answers. It is about you finding your truth. Where you are now in your journey sets the stage for where you go next. We use four steps in helping you discover how each principle serves you on this journey. Since most spiritual seeking begins in recognizing our emptiness, or in bottoming out, the first step is Step 0: Readiness; Step 1. The True Self; Step 2. Soul Surgery; and Step 3. Love as the Way. These truths are touchstones. You might take time yearly as a tune up, when you experience a dark night of the soul, or have forgotten your "why". Purposefully creating a life of authenticity, of integrity and self-efficacy takes time. You are worth it.

I once read a biography of Mary McLeod Bethune, an African American woman who was determined to create a school for young black girls in 1904. Mrs. Bethune has become a spirit member on my "Board of Directors". Her theory on teaching someone a new skill or learning a new skill yourself involved three essential steps. First, you make the effort to teach the mind: examine your assumptions and beliefs (thoughts). Second, the heart: the place of your hopes, dreams, and desires (spiritual). Third, the hands: how will you apply your new learning to life (action). In some circles we call this "whole body learning"!

Three images showed up in my spirit as I approached the venture of creating The Journey to You Center Oracle. Each image that appeared represents one of the steps involved in Mary McLeod Bethune's teaching that became my guide. As the image of a Crown appeared it reminded me to become aware of my thoughts. Learning something new requires adjustments in thinking. An image of a tree called me to my roots, asking: was I rooted in my heart? An image of a hand represented the call to action, A new belief must be transformed into a new behavior. This practice of grounding in Mary McLeod Bethune's wisdom became the touchstone that I would reflect on as I drew and painted and wrote. Spirit showed up and what I had learned in reflecting on my life and through my work with others transformed into 36 spiritual truths, 4 steps, and hence, 40 days of journaling your way to the heart of your being where your truth resides.

Travel Tips

CONSIDERING A CHALLENGING JOURNEY TAKES willingness and emotional muscle. It takes a hunger for something more. Are you ready to make the effort to sustain the self-love that leads to peace? Identification and letting go of unnecessary baggage take consistent commitment. Willingness is required to try different ways. A travel buddy is ideal. Traveling accessories include light (Spirit), food, i.e., (Information, maps, your music), and lastly, courage and desire to adapt to and adopt universal tools that will be presented along the way. Go forth and manifest!

The Journey

0. Readiness

Before your journey begins, describe your "current situation".

Q. Describe your *desire* for change?

Q. What will change cost?

Jackie Smith-Jefferson

1. Your true self.

All problems arise as a result of forgetting who you are. Establishing *priorities* in your life will allow you to be *true to yourself*. It will increase your ability to live *consciously* as well. Mind your foundation.

Q. In the course, of your day, where is most of your time and energy spent?

Q. In what areas of life do you experience confusion, discord, confirmation, peace of mind?

Jackie Smith-Jefferson

_____

_____

_____

_____

_____

_____

_____

_____

_____

_____

_____

_____

_____

_____

_____

_____

2. Soul surgery.

The work of spiritual warriors takes a courageous heart. "The bravest thing you can do is tell yourself the *truth*..." Akansha Chopra

Q. What core beliefs do you hold to be true in the major areas of life?

Q. What is most important to you?

Jackie Smith-Jefferson

3. Love as the way.

To navigate this *authenticity* of self, we tell ourselves the truth about what we are willing to *do*, what are we willing to *let go*. Many want to fast forward through the process. But it is in the *process* that we practice our tools, hence, manifesting our destiny.

Q. What are your heart's purest desires?

Jackie Smith-Jefferson

I

Image of the Crowned Head

THE FIRST CHANNEL THROUGH WHICH we will learn or re-establish our path is mentally. "First things First" is an organizational tool. First things govern the rest.

1. The Supreme Power in the Universe has many names, including God, The *Divine*, Supreme Being, Great Creator, Father God, Mother Earth, Yahweh, Higher Power, Holy Spirit, Healing Angels, *Higher Self*, G.O.D. Humans have been given free will to make *choices*. Partnering with the Supreme Power is most effective in this business called life.

Q. As you look over your day examine your dominant thoughts throughout the day to ascertain what you *worshipped* today. Write about it.

Q. What thoughts bring peace?

Jackie Smith-Jefferson

2. This Supreme Power is LOVE. *Love* is the reason for being, it is the Way and the Way maker. The assignment, one might say. We are born of pure Divine love and we will return to love.

Q. How do you define love?

Q. Give some examples and or experiences of pure love.

Jackie Smith-Jefferson

3. It is God's will for us to have life and have it abundantly. Hold out your hands, open your heart to receive this gift. Love life with all your being and life will love you back. This is the *law of Attraction*.

Q. What is your reaction to the idea of God's will for us described above?

Q. What have you been taught about God's expectations of us?

Jackie Smith-Jefferson

_____

_____

_____

_____

_____

_____

_____

_____

_____

_____

_____

_____

_____

_____

_____

_____

_____

4. We are one with God, with all creation and all people. There is a *universal spirit* that runs through all. What we do in life has a ripple effect. What you choose to share, negative or positive, will take root for generations to come.

Q. How do you feel about your connection to the Divine and to the rest of *humankind*?

Q. When do you most feel this connection?

Jackie Smith-Jefferson

5. Every person is a unique expression of God. We were all born with a *nature* that is divine and our purpose is to express our divine potential.

Q. What about yourself can you believe is divine?

Q. What challenges arise for you in seeing the divine in others?

Jackie Smith-Jefferson

_____

_____

_____

_____

_____

_____

_____

_____

_____

_____

_____

_____

_____

_____

_____

_____

6. Prayer and meditation heighten our awareness of God, our awareness of our surroundings, our *awareness* of our place in the universe. Its benefits are numerous. A Zen proverb states, "Meditate for 20 minutes if you have time. If you don't have time, meditate for an hour!" Simply set aside time to practice silence. Breathing deeply, affirm that all is well. Ground your soul in the here and now! There are as many ways as there are individuals to do this.

Q. Have there been blocks to the idea of stillness?

Q. Name ways you have practiced being present to the moment?

Jackie Smith-Jefferson

7. Our *thoughts* create our experiences. In this way they act as an Oracle. However, we have the *power* to choose our thoughts. If you want to know what you believe, look at your life. Therein lies the manifestation of your thinking.

Q. What are some core beliefs that ring true for you about God, yourself, relationships?

Q. Which of your relationships reflect your core beliefs and which are in conflict?

Jackie Smith-Jefferson

8. Our purpose is to express our potential as a child of God. We are here to be of *service*. Each *talent* we've been given has worth. They must be used or we will lose them and so will the universe.

Q. What talents have you been given, inherited?

Q. How do you demonstrate their value to yourself and to the world around you?

Jackie Smith-Jefferson

9. We have a *sacred* responsibility to make a positive difference in the world. In your home and your community, you are to *model* your truth. Inaction can be harmful to your soul and a loss for your community.

Q. What do you feel the most passion about?

Q. How do you create balance between your passions and your responsibilities?

10. God is the *source* of our supply---of Love, talent, joy, peace! Neither money, significant others, jobs nor ourselves are the source. I can choose to *partner* with God, recognizing from whence my good comes from and receive with *Holy ease.* Or I can force solutions based on my fears, illusions and fantasies which inevitably backfire.

Q. Describe an experience when having your way backfired?

Q. Describe times you've experienced the Holy ease of cooperating with Spirit.

Jackie Smith-Jefferson

11. Understanding through study, reflection, and using the teachings of Jesus and other Avatars from other world religions can transform our lives. They all teach strikingly similar lessons. They are all consistent in their efforts toward the quest for love.

Q. Identify the times, people, and areas of your life where it's easy to see love?

Q. What are some life's areas where more love would benefit all involved?

Jackie Smith-Jefferson

12. There are many paths to The One. What works for one person may not work for another. The soul yearns for a spiritual practice that is *tailor made*.

Q. What are some of the ways you have practiced opening your heart and your mind?

Q. What ideas are you *willing* to "try on"?

Jackie Smith-Jefferson

II

Image of the Heart Shaped Tree with Deep Roots

MY RELATIONSHIP WITH OTHERS IS directly affected by my relationship with myself. My relationship with myself will be the source of my *serenity* or dis-ease. Being rooted in the heart is a game changer. Where we are rooted determines the fruit we will bear.

1. In order to find the solution, I must first *admit* the problem. Our *journey* includes hills, valleys, tests, perceived conspiracies, dark caves and crevices, pink clouds, and victories. Some of my travel mates have used the Serenity Prayer as a map to the truth.

Q. What are some of the *"assignments"*, and emotional challenges that have presented themselves to you lately?

Q. Which of these challenges are yours to address?

2. I *trust* my process. My process began with *hope* turning into *faith* which then grew into trust. Hope is the one thing that we must carry throughout life's challenges and the toughest of times. And it is hope that will build the most strength.

Q. Give examples of self-deception on the path to Higher Consciousness.

Q. Look back over your life and describe the strength built during trying times.

Jackie Smith-Jefferson

3. I decide daily to *partner* with The One.

As you make a daily conscious decision to partner with God/Spirit/Source on this perilous journey of life you will notice what is called Holy ease vs the chaos and confusion resulting from ego driven choices.

Q. What are you willing to *surrender*?

Q. What are some decisions you can make today?

4. I look at my life with clear eyes. While examining your choices, your actions, your thoughts, and feelings, look squarely at your part in creating your reality. This is the work of a spiritual warrior.

Q. What is the *reality* you're experiencing right now?

Q. Describe your choices, your actions, your thoughts, and feelings, that have led to that reality.

5. I process the *effectiveness* of my choices... alone, with God/Spirit/Source and a nonjudgmental soul. "Confession is good for the soul". It is wise to choose worthy guides along the path with which you feel safe to reveal your true self.

Q. What are some characteristics of a *worthy* soul to trust with your testimony?

Q. However, many times you can, complete this statement:

I trust _____.

Jackie Smith-Jefferson

6. I make *ready* for change. Consequences of our actions contain grist for the soul. In order for the soul to *evolve*, we must pass through levels of awareness. Readiness occurs when we *sense* the discord in our heart and mind.

Q. Which of your characteristics repeatedly bring on discomfort, dis-ease, guilt, misunderstandings, confusion?

Q. Which characteristics are you *invested* in releasing and which are you not?

Jackie Smith-Jefferson

7. I ask The One for help. The journey of a spiritual warrior is not for wimps. It takes courage to face and respect your strengths and your weaknesses.

Q. What are your strengths and your weaknesses?

Q. What are your beliefs about asking for help?

Jackie Smith-Jefferson

8. I *account* for my part in offenses I experienced, hence contributed to. Relationships with other humans require us to be open, honest, willing to be wrong and to acknowledge that it takes two. Acknowledging that may feel like we're removing ground glass from our *psyche*. Acknowledging that may feel like we're removing ground glass from our psyche.

Q. What actions are needed to stay current in my primary relationships?

Q. What relationship needs closure?

9. I *own* my part in the offenses, making right my wrongs. *Amending* your part in the problems of your life is necessary to achieve peace. A practice of steadfast, *honorable* behavior brings trust, respect and even intimacy in relationships, especially with self.

Q. What behaviors have contributed to dissension in your life?

Q. Which ones help to create peace and harmony?

Jackie Smith-Jefferson

10. I practice daily *self-reflection*, choosing actions that reflect my truest self. As spiritual beings on this human path, we fall, hopefully without judgment, we dust ourselves off and get back in the game. At the end of our day we search our heart.

Q. Am I creating or dismantling peace and harmony today? Give specific references.

Q. A fully lived life must, by definition, include mistakes. How might that influence you in the Journey to Your Center Oracle?

Jackie Smith-Jefferson

11. As I draw closer to The One, I draw closer to myself. This path leads to greater joy, unbounded freedom and an increased awareness of the rich bounty that is our inheritance.

Q. Where, when, and with whom do you feel closest to God?

Q. What happens when you take the time to *commune* with Spirit?

Jackie Smith-Jefferson

_____

12. I pass the blessing on. To live in our community is to be a *part of* it. Apathy kills the soul. As human beings we have an innate need to connect and support one another.

Q. Are you open when someone *reaches out* to ask you for support? Are you open to asking for support?

Q. If an opportunity were to present itself to give hope to a hopeless soul, what would you share with this human.

Jackie Smith-Jefferson

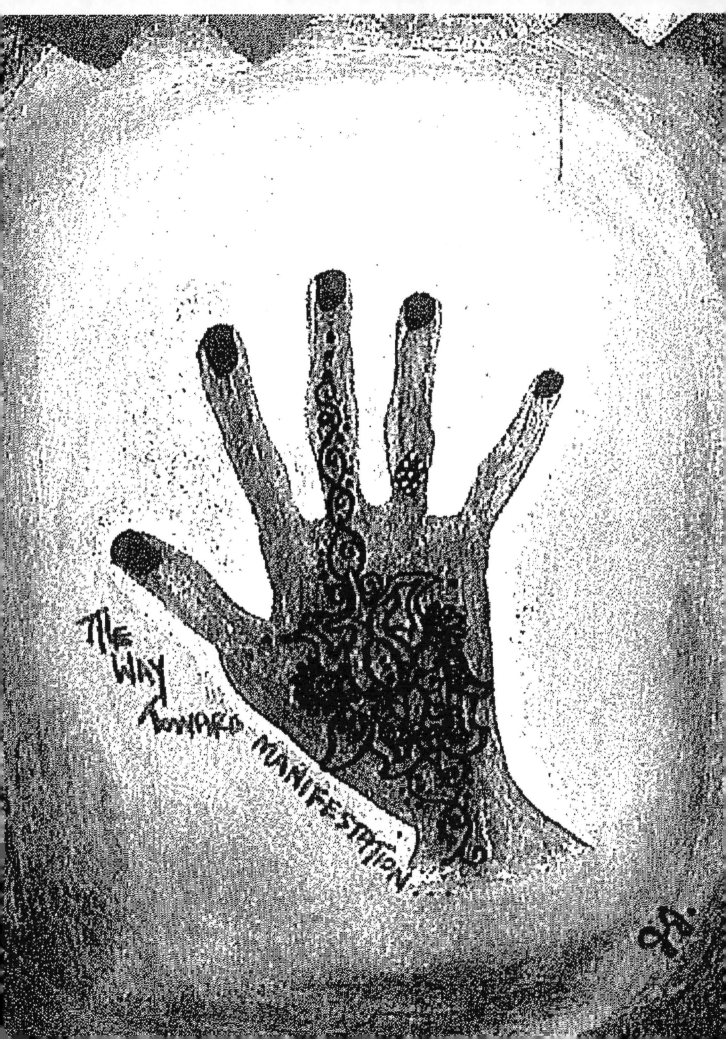

III

Image of Hennaed Hand

THIS IS WHERE WE EXHIBIT concrete actions that *demonstrate* our *ideals*. Ideals are important, but like intentions, if they aren't grounded in behavior, they are just up there somewhere in your head. *Building* new skills takes repeated action. Action builds momentum, empowers, and leads to confidence. Practicing together with others leads to honorable relationship skills.

1. I maintain a *balance* between my importance, and the *greater good*. *Peace* begins and ends with me. As part of a larger community, all voices must be heard.

Q. Do you give everyone the same respect you desire for yourself (even when it's not reciprocated)?

Q. What are some of your core beliefs regarding respect for self and others?

Jackie Smith-Jefferson

2. I practice divine order in all my affairs

For some this is God, self, then others. Remember who gets the oxygen mask first when on a plane? When I put first things first, all else falls into place. Taking care to build a strong *foundation* blesses all that follows.

Q. Within a 24-hour day, what is "first things first" for you?

Q. List your top 5 priorities in life, in order.

Jackie Smith-Jefferson

3. As I grow to *accept* my process, I learn to accept others process as well. I lead with *honor.* We did not get the way we are overnight. It took great discomfort to build the willingness to change negative patterns and then it takes time to outgrow them.

Q. What has blocked patience with yours and others process?

Q. Along the way, how have you shown compassion for yourself and others on this journey?

4. I am *100%* accountable for my part. As I take on more freedom, I take on more responsibility. Being accountable for my part leads to autonomy and makes being a part of the whole possible. Consciously being a part of the whole, I govern my own actions and accept the natural consequences for them.

Q. What does it mean to hold up your end of the deal?

Q. Where have my beliefs and behaviors regarding belonging or being a part of, led me in my life?

5. My primary *purpose* is to carry a message of hope in all my affairs. I personally believe that hope is a choice I make, a muscle I *exercise* and a staple in my spiritual cupboard. How else are we able to show up, role model it and share it when needed? Wherever we are in our journey, we could all use some.

Q. Are there blocks to focusing on the good/God in others?

Q. In what current situation can I practice seeing the good?

6. Spiritual growth, mine, and others, is priority. M. Scott Peck said, "Love is the *will* to extend one's self for the purpose of *nurturing* one's own or another's spiritual growth." I examine my level of *integrity* each day by lining up my beliefs and actions. This habit of checking our *intention* against our behavior is key in developing healthy relationships.

Q. When you follow an unsatisfying action or behavior down to its roots, what insight can you gain?

Q. As you gain insight, how can you meet it with compassion?

Jackie Smith-Jefferson

7. It is my choice to be happy or not. I am responsible for my wellbeing. *Interdependence* blesses me with the *dignity* to be me and the *self -esteem* that comes from taking care of me while doing my part in relationship to others.

Q. What are some spiritual, mental, emotional, physical, and financial blessings that I've gained because of taking responsibility for myself?

Jackie Smith-Jefferson

8. I give *unconditionally*; else the strings attached will destroy the *gift*. I share what was so freely given to me.

Q. Give personal examples of spiritual giving, enabling, bribing, and taking care of business?

Q. Describe the last time you had an opportunity to share with compassion and without expectations of payback.

Jackie Smith-Jefferson

9. My employer is a loving God. As I conduct my social behavior according to spiritual principles, I develop the spirit of service. We share the workload with God. Hence, we are in partnership with God. When God/The One/Spirit is leading the way, we *navigate* through responsibilities in a spirit of *stewardship*.

Q. In what situations have I found it a). hard, b). easy to conduct my social behavior according to spiritual *principles*?

Jackie Smith-Jefferson

10. Learning to "*Live* and *let Live*" is *freedom*.

When facing conflict, it is wise to practice asking yourself, "Do I have a dog in this race?", "How important is it to have the last word". "Do you want to be right or free?"

Q. What areas of your life are ripe for controversy?

Q. When faced with controversy, what have you learned about yourself and others that is helpful in practicing effective communication?

Jackie Smith-Jefferson

11. I will *be* the *change* I want to see in others. My best sermon is the *example* I set. As Albert Schweitzer said, "Example is not the main thing in influencing others. It is the only thing." Maladaptive tools i.e., criticism, advice giving, spouting opinions, "shoulding" and nagging are all counterproductive, especially if you are not practicing what you preach.

Q. Describe a personal experience where you have been the recipient or the instigator of each one of these maladaptive "tools".

Q. In the spirit of setting an example of how you would like to be addressed, write a letter to a significant person in your life that is *empowering* and *respectful*.

12. I will treat others with *respect* and *dignity*. We are all one *tribe*. *Creating* a sense of *safety* with others through *humility*, leads to *mutual* trust. *Trust* leads to respect. When we are *open-minded* towards others, we can all be teachers, role models.

Q. Describe a time you experienced a sense of safety and dignity because of someone's approach to you?

Q. Describe how you would practice this approach with a new co-worker, a new acquaintance, a child, or your partner?

Jackie Smith-Jefferson

Wrapping Things Up

AND SO, WE'VE COME TO the end of this workbook. Begin your own Journey to your Center, your own Oracle. Thank you for your honesty and perseverance in doing the work. I pray these tools will bless you, keep you focused and give you the sustenance you need to "stay true to thine self" on this scenic, winding and sometimes arduous road called life. May your way be lit with love and truth from likeminded souls to guide you along the way. Namaste!

About the Author

JACKIE SMITH- JEFFERSON WAS BORN in Austin, Tx. raised in Nashville, Tn. and is currently living in Mobile, Ala. In previous chapters of her life, she served as a dancer, a choreographer, a soldier in the U.S. Army, a wife of a soldier and mother, a counselor, teacher, mentor, an R. & B., Blues and Jazz entertainer and musician in various bands singing her own blend of uplifting blue funky jazz from historic Printers Alley and New thought churches, and treatment centers to Jenna Bush's wedding, Jackie has graced stages nationally and internationally. She now travels where spirit leads as a metaphysical minister, using her talents in music, and story telling in her one woman presentation, "Soul Stories." Her heart is in raising her own consciousness to embrace its Divinity and being a catalyst for love and truth in others, beginning with her family. During the 1950s, she grew up in a diversified household environment with parents, Kitty (activist/journalist) and Wm. O. Smith (jazz musician/educator and Nashville music legend). With late night jam sessions with the likes of Dizzy Gillespie, Coleman Hawkins and Cab Calloway, and her mother's daytime activist meetings, her childhood home was a melting pot of people from ALL corners of Nashville coming together to participate in creating and enjoying good music and a stronger community of forward minded folk during a time of separation in the south based on the Jim Crow Laws. Celebration, stewardship and sharing of her time, and resources from Father/Mother God is in her DNA.

Her audiences have included truth seekers, those seeking freedom from self-made shackles, and who have forgotten their way. As a spiritual warrior, she has the ability to reach the soul of her audience through her authenticity, just the right question, recognition of our oneness, humor, transparency and always a classic song thrown in for good measure. The Journey to Your Center Oracle was deposited into her soul in 2016 and grew into a visual and oral testament to her own journey. Enjoy!

Printed in the United States
By Bookmasters